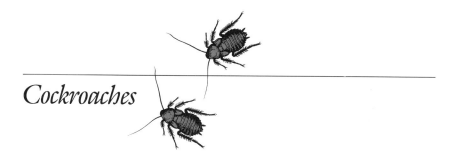

Cockroaches

COCKROACHES

MONA KERBY

Franklin Watts   New York   London   Toronto   Sydney   A First Book   1989

ILLUSTRATIONS BY ANNE CANEVARI GREEN

Photographs courtesy of: Animals/Animals: pp. 3 (Bates
Littlehales), 14, 17 (R. A. Mendez) 25 (Holt Studios), 29
(Oxford Scientific Films), 32 (E.R. Degginger), 36, 42
(R.A. Mendez), 46 (bottom, John Pontier); Bruce
Coleman: pp. 38 (Kim Taylor), 47 (top, C.B. Frith;
bottom, Kim Taylor); Photo Researchers: pp. 40 (Fred
McConnaughey), 46 (top, Norma Thomas; center,
Harry Rogers); Peter Arnold: p. 44 (Alan Morgan).

Library of Congress Cataloging-in-Publication Data

Kerby, Mona.
Cockroaches.

(A First book)
Bibliography: p.
Includes index.
Summary: Examines the body parts, behavior, and likes
and dislikes of one of the oldest creatures in the world.
1. Cockroaches — Juvenile literature. [1. Cockroaches]
I. Green, Anne Canevari, Ill.   II. Title.   III. Series.
QL505.5.K47   1989   595.7'22   88-37857
ISBN 0-531-10689-6

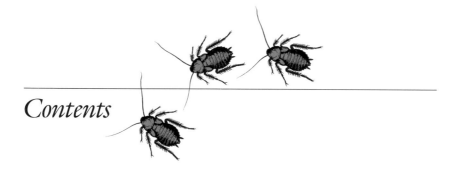

Contents

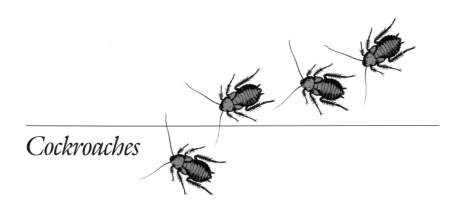

Cockroaches

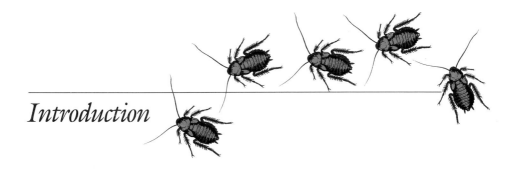

Introduction

Imagine, for a moment, that you are a time traveler. You step into your time machine and set it to travel backwards in time—350 million years ago.

Suddenly there is a whirlwind of activity. Lights on the control panel are flashing. Motors are humming. Data are spewing from the computer printer. Everything is wildly vibrating.

And then all is quiet. You open the door and step out. The air is moist and humid. You are surrounded by masses of tree ferns and evergreens. Plants are everywhere. There are no dinosaurs, and there won't be any for several hundred million years. And of course, there are no humans. Glancing down, you recognize something that you've seen in your own time. What is it?

It's a cockroach.

For at least 350 million years, cockroaches have been living on earth. They are one of the oldest insects in the world. Cockroaches are 100 times older than humans.

You, the time traveler, have just stepped into the age of cockroaches. Here, there are more cockroaches than all other winged insects combined. Cockroaches are the dominant insects.

This time in the earth's history was known as the *Carboniferous period*. The lush vegetation eventually formed the great coal beds. Scientists have discovered fossils of these early cockroaches in the coal measures of Kansas, Illinois, Great Britain, Germany, and France.

After examining these fossils, it is clear that cockroaches have not changed much in all that time. Today, their wings are smaller and are shaped a little differently. Female cockroaches no longer have a visible sword-shaped ovipositor, which enables them to pierce the ground to lay eggs. Now, the ovipositor is completely internal.

But, other than that, cockroaches' bodies are pretty much the same. They still like moist conditions, and they can go for long periods of time without food or water. In modern times, cockroaches have managed to develop a resistance to pesticides. Somehow, these simple insects have endured and flourished for hundreds of millions of years.

1

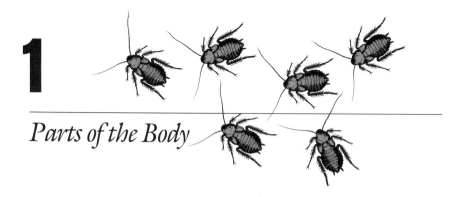

Parts of the Body

Try to kill a cockroach as it scurries across your kitchen floor. It isn't easy.

Some insects have specialized body parts which help them live and work. Such parts include long tongues for sipping nectar, wings designed for long flights, legs that are made for jumping, and stingers for defense against enemies.

But there's nothing really unique about a cockroach's body. Still, you may not be convinced of that fact when one of those little rascals gets away. It seems that the cockroach is an expert at escape.

To a certain extent, a cockroach's body does protect it from enemies. The cockroach's exoskeleton, like that of all insects, is similar to a knight's suit of armor. Flat, oval-shaped, and coated with wax, a cockroach can slip through a crack that is no wider than a matchstick. Furthermore, the wax waterproofs the cockroach. It can stay under water for ten or fifteen minutes without drowning.

As with all insects, the cockroach's exoskeleton is divided into three sections: the head, the *thorax,* and the *abdomen.* Organs in these sections alert the cockroach to danger and allow it to flee quickly.

Head

A cockroach often keeps its small head tilted under its body and hidden by the thorax. Without a doubt, the most prominent features on the head are the *antennae.* The antennae are almost always longer than the body and they move constantly, in whiplike fashion. These two tubes are each composed of 130 segments. Thousands of sense receptors are located on the antennae. With them, the cockroach has the ability to taste, smell, and touch. The cockroach also uses them to detect moisture in the air and its direction. For these reasons, the antennae are even more important to the cockroach than its eyes.

The large compound eyes are on top of the head behind the antennae and are composed of many small facets. Occasionally the cockroach may also have two simple eyes that are near the antennae sockets.

EXTERNAL STRUCTURES

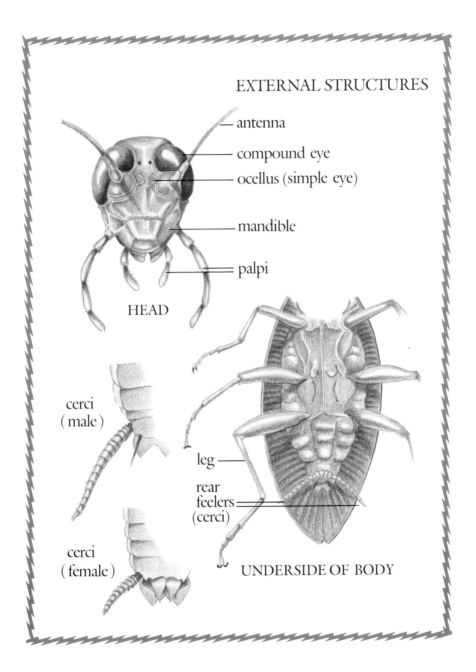

— antenna

— compound eye

— ocellus (simple eye)

— mandible

— palpi

HEAD

cerci
(male)

cerci
(female)

leg ——

rear
feelers
(cerci)

UNDERSIDE OF BODY

The head of Periplaneta australasiae,
the Australian cockroach.
The antennae are a prominent feature.

The mouth parts allow the cockroach to eat nearly anything. The mouth parts are able to bite, chew, and lick. The strong, toothed *mandibles* crush food and chew sideways. The hypopharynx, or tongue, is used to lick food.

Perhaps the most interesting features of the mouth are the *palpi*. These four feelers are always moving and touching things. Both pairs—one pair is longer than the other—are studded with bristles. A cockroach uses its palpi to taste food before it places the food in its mouth. As a result, a cockroach can taste poison without eating it. Now that's a handy trick to have when a cockroach lives near humans.

Thorax

The wings and legs are attached to the large, rounded thorax. With those species of cockroaches that have wings, there are two pairs. The top pair are called the *tegmina* (forewings). In addition to being translucent, the tegmina are somewhat hardened. The *hindwings* are more delicate. They are also shorter than the tegmina. Most pest cockroaches don't fly when they are trying to escape. If they do, the flight is a short, fluttering hop. In order to make a quick getaway, cockroaches depend on their legs.

Their six legs are slender and are almost equal in length. The first segments of each leg are folded underneath the cockroach's body. The rest of the legs are visible on either side of the body and are covered with stiff hairs. Two claws are on each foot. The hairs and claws help a cockroach to hold on to most surfaces. Also important to the leg are the knee joints. They are so sensitive to vibrations that they can detect the footstep of another cockroach.

Abdomen

The largest section of the cockroach is the *abdomen*. The abdomen resembles a suit of armor because it is composed of small, hard, overlapping segments. The *tergites* are on the topside, under the wings. The segments that are on the underside of the cockroach are called *sternites*. Both the tergites and the sternites are able to expand and contract.

Two short, unjointed *styles* are on the rear ends of male cockroaches. (They are also on the *nymphs,* the newly hatched cockroaches, of both sexes.) The styles help males to mate with females.

Found on the rear ends of both the male and the female cockroach are two jointed, sticklike appendages called the *cerci.* The cerci are extraordinarily sensitive to

The underside of the
Australian cockroach. The
antennae, six legs, and
cerci are clearly visible.

vibrations, sound, and air movements. Such a distur-
bance immediately triggers the cerci to flash nerve impulses to the legs.

Have you ever turned on a kitchen light and discovered cockroaches scurrying away? It wasn't the light that
startled them. On the contrary, the cockroaches "felt"
you coming with their cerci. As soon as cockroaches
perceive an enemy, they are off and running in fifty-four
one-thousandths of a second, faster than you can blink
an eye.

Internal Anatomy

If you think about it, you are similar to a cockroach in
many ways. Both you and the cockroach have eyes and
legs. Both of you run and rest. And, you also enjoy
some of the very same foods.

Moreover, a cockroach is similar to you on the inside of its body. It, too, has a heart and a brain. It has
blood and it breathes air. But a cockroach does have
distinct differences from a human. Isn't it wonderful to
know that your mother will never mistake you for a
cockroach!

If you have ever seen a freshly squashed cockroach,
you are already aware of one major characteristic. The
white squishy stuff is called *fat body*. Fat body is a white
tissue that fills most of the body cavity. In some ways it

18

INTERNAL STRUCTURES

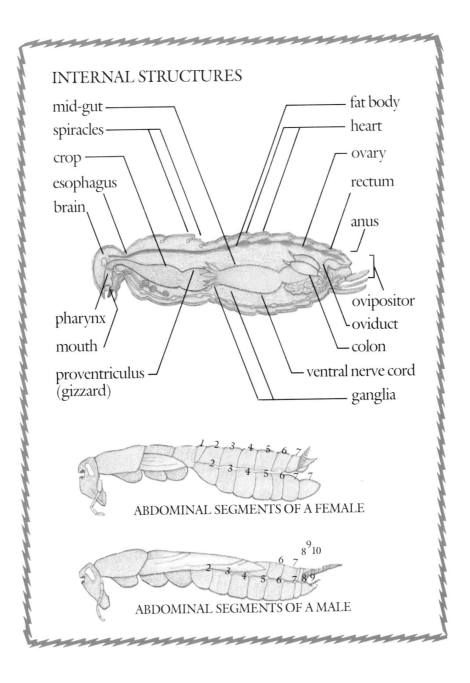

mid-gut

spiracles

crop

esophagus

brain

fat body

heart

ovary

rectum

anus

pharynx

mouth

proventriculus
(gizzard)

ovipositor

oviduct

colon

ventral nerve cord

ganglia

ABDOMINAL SEGMENTS OF A FEMALE

ABDOMINAL SEGMENTS OF A MALE

19

is like our liver. Nutrients are stored there. Proteins are synthesized by the fat body and secreted to the blood.

The blood of a cockroach is clear. Our blood is red because it transports oxygen to our body parts. Cockroach blood does not contain oxygen. This clear fluid moves freely throughout the body cavity, carrying nutrients to tissues and organs and carrying wastes to the excretory organs. The blood is pumped by the heart, which is in the dorsal (top) side of the abdomen.

A cockroach does not breathe like you because it doesn't have a nose. Instead, a cockroach breathes through ten pairs of holes called *spiracles*. Two pairs are located on top of the thorax. Eight pairs are on the sides of the abdomen. All of the spiracles have a closing device which prevents water loss. Inside the body of the cockroach, the spiracles are attached to the tracheal system. This network of tubes carries oxygen to all parts of the insect.

The brain, the *ventral nerve cord,* and its *ganglia* compose the central nervous system. Impulses to this system cause a cockroach to run when disturbed and to eat food that it likes. A brain is not as important to a cockroach as it is to you. Scientists have discovered that a cockroach can continue about its business without one.

Finally, a cockroach digests its food differently from you. After the food is crushed by the mouth parts, it passes into the *crop*. Here, most of the digestion occurs. The crop is capable of stretching so that it can hold large amounts. The *proventriculus,* or *gizzard,* further crushes the food and then passes it on to the mid-*gut,* where many of the nutrients are absorbed. The hind gut removes the water from the digested food and then discharges dry, hard pellets of waste.

2

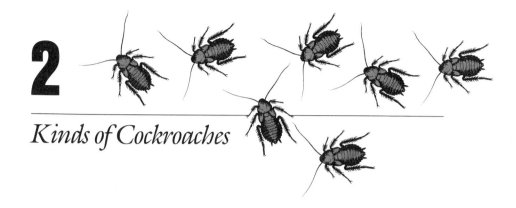

Kinds of Cockroaches

Did you know that there are 3,500 known species, or kinds, of cockroaches? What's more, scientists believe that there are still thousands of species that have not yet been named.

The suborder for cockroaches is *Blattaria,* which means "to shun the light." But most people don't use this term. Instead, they call them by their nicknames. The word *cockroach* comes from the Spanish word *cucaracha,* which means "crazy bug." Two other names for cockroaches are water bugs and black beetles. Somehow, it's easier for people to admit that they have water bugs in their house than it is for them to say that they have cockroaches.

People in certain geographical areas will occasionally name cockroaches for other groups of people. (It's not really a compliment to have a cockroach named after you.) For example, in Nova Scotia, cockroaches are called "Yankee Settlers." East Germans call them "Russians," and West Germans call them "French" cockroaches. In fact, the major pest cockroaches—the American, German, Oriental, and Australian cockroaches—are not even native to those areas. They are all originally from Africa.

Unfortunately (or fortunately), you will never see most of the 3,500 cockroach species that roam the earth, for they live in tropical forests, far away from humans. Some of these are large and brilliantly colored.

Believe it or not, fewer than thirty-five species are associated with people. These particular cockroaches don't live near people because they like us. It's just that our food and shelter attract them. Fifty-seven different cockroach species are known to exist in the United States. The state of Texas has thirty-two different kinds of cockroaches, more than any other state. (One Texas cockroach, nearly 2 inches long, is now on display at the Smithsonian.)

In this chapter, you will learn about cockroaches that you are likely to find where you live. After you read this chapter, you will be able to call cockroaches by their correct, scientific names.

IDENTIFICATION KEY OF COCKROACH PESTS

Scientific Name and Common Name	Characteristics	Size
Blatta orientalis or Oriental cockroach	Black to very dark brown, females wingless, males reduced wings	Average 17–29 mm
Blattella germanica or German cockroach	Tan, full wings	Small 10–15 mm
Leucophaea maderae or Madeira cockroach	Olive, full wings mottled with dark lines	Very large 40–50 mm
Periplaneta americana or American cockroach	Reddish-brown, pale yellow edge on thorax, full wings	Large 29–44 mm
Periplaneta australasiae or Australian cockroach	Reddish brown, pale yellow edge on thorax, yellow on edge of full wings	Large 29–44 mm
Periplaneta fuliginosa or Smoky brown cockroach	Brownish black, full wings	Large 29–44 mm
Supella longipalpa or Brown-banded cockroach	Tan, with brown bands, full wings	Small 10–15 mm

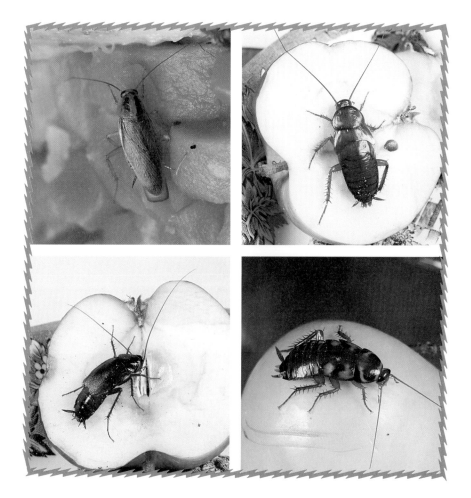

Top left and right: Blattella germanica
(German cockroach); Periplaneta americana
(American cockroach); Bottom left and right:
Blatta orientalis *(Oriental cockroach)*; Peri-
planeta australasiae *(Australian cockroach)*

25

Blattella germanica,
or German Cockroach

The German cockroach, sometimes known as a Steam Fly or Croton Bug, is found in all parts of the world. It is the most commonly found species in homes, on planes, and on ships. In fact, the German cockroach has been described as the world's most successful commercial traveler.

If you have cockroaches, they are probably German cockroaches. These cockroaches like heat and moisture. Although they are found in bathrooms, they prefer kitchens. You will find them in cabinets, near water pipes, under moist sinks, in stoves, and behind refrigerators.

The German cockroach is the smallest of the pest species and measures from ½ inches to ⅝ inches long. It can squeeze through a crack that is a sixteenth of an inch wide. Its body is a tan, brownish-yellow color. Two dark streaks run lengthwise down the back. Both the female and male have wings. However, the female's wings are longer and cover the length of the abdomen.

On the average, a female produces seven *ootheca,* or egg cases, in her lifetime. Each of the ootheca remains attached to the female's body for about twenty days. At that time, the thirty to forty-eight eggs hatch. The young cockroaches mature in a little over a month. Once German cockroaches reach adulthood, they will live for four or five months.

Blatta orientalis,
or Oriental Cockroach

The Oriental cockroach, or black beetle, is also a world-wide pest. It is the most common pest in Great Britain, and, with the exception of the most northern parts, it is found all over the United States.

While German cockroaches like a warm temperature, Oriental cockroaches prefer a cooler one. They are frequently found in basements, cellars, and in bathrooms, near toilets, bathtubs, and sinks. Many of them live in the sewers and enter houses through sewage drains. During the summer months, Oriental cockroaches are often seen out-of-doors, near homes and trash dumps. They can tolerate a hot, dry climate as long as they have access to water.

Oriental cockroaches are ⅝ inches to 1¼ inches in length. They are reddish brown to black. Neither females nor males are able to fly. Males' wings do not cover the abdomen. Most females don't have wings. If they do, the wings are extremely short.

There may be as many as eighteen eggs in each ootheca. At 62° F (18° C), the ootheca will hatch in a little more than a month. In unheated buildings, however, it may take as long as a year for the ootheca to hatch. In favorable conditions, males reach the adult stage within five months. It takes females approximately nine months to mature.

Periplaneta americana,
or American Cockroach

Nicknames for the American cockroach include palmetto bug, Bombay canary, and water bug. As with the German cockroach, the American cockroach is found worldwide—in places such as India, the southern United States, New York, and the coal mines of Wales.

American cockroaches are generally seen during the months of July and August. They, too, prefer a warm, moist environment. Basements, water pipes, bathrooms, and sewers are choice locations. They are a common pest of restaurants, bakeries, and grocery stores.

The American cockroach is large. It measures from $1\frac{1}{8}$ inches to $1\frac{3}{4}$ inches. The body is a shiny reddish brown with a pale yellow color on its thorax. The wings of the male extend well past the tip of the abdomen. The female's wings barely overlap the abdomen. With their fully developed wings, both sexes can fly short distances, but they rarely do.

After a successful mating, an ootheca develops in about a week. Once an ootheca has formed, it does not remain attached to the female cockroach's body. Instead, she deposits it somewhere. Approximately sixteen eggs are in each ootheca. In warm weather, the eggs develop in about a month and hatch two months later. In colder climates, this process takes longer. Within six to twelve

Two American cockroach nymphs of different ages are shown here with an adult on the right.

29

months, the young cockroaches mature. Adult cockroaches live for about a year.

Other Species

There are other species that are considered pests by humans. One of these is the Australian cockroach *(Periplaneta australasiae)*. It somewhat resembles the American cockroach in coloring, though the Australian is a little smaller than the American. The Australian cockroach thrives in warm climates such as Africa, Ecuador, Puerto Rico, Bermuda, and the West Indies. It is the most troublesome cockroach in Florida. In cooler climates, the Australian cockroach thrives in the warm, moist environments of greenhouses.

Another major pest species is the smoky brown cockroach *(Periplaneta fuliginosa)*. This cockroach is a shiny, brownish black and is abundant in the southern states, particularly Georgia, northern Florida, and Texas. It is commonly found in garages, outbuildings, and woodpiles. At night, it flies to porch lights. In Houston, Texas, the smoky brown cockroach buzzes streetlights.

In the last forty years, the brown-banded cockroach *(Supella longipalpa)* has rapidly multiplied and has been found in every state except Vermont. Similar in size to the German cockroach, this small cockroach (³⁄₈ inches to ½ inches) has two brown bands crossing its back. It is active, tends to fly when disturbed, and often flies around the lights in houses. Brown-banded cockroaches are frequently found in bathrooms. They generally cluster together in closets, drawers, piles of clothes, inside books, and behind wallpaper, where they eat the paste.

Perhaps the most repulsive species is the Asian cockroach *(Blattella asahinai)*. While similar in size and appearance to the German cockroach, it is disgustingly different.

Called flying roaches by news reporters, flights of Asian cockroaches have been measured up to 120 feet (37 m), the distance of the Wright brothers' first flight. They are attracted to light and are not afraid of people. They fly toward TV sets and they especially like to roost on someone wearing white. Thousands of them will hover on walls. Outside, they fly up like grasshoppers and cluster on the ground so compactly that a person can step on twenty-five or thirty at once.

Asian cockroaches first appeared in Florida in 1984 and were probably stowaways on a ship from southeast Asia. Within two years, they covered 400 to 500 square miles (1,036–1,295 sq km). Because they reproduce rapidly and frequently "hitchhike," Asian cockroaches are expected to migrate to the rest of the United States.

One of the more interesting pests is the Madeira cockroach *(Leucophaea maderae)*. Long established in Cuba, Jamaica, Puerto Rico, and the Bahamas, in recent

Recently arrived in the United States
is the Asian cockroach—and it flies.

years it has become a pest in New York City buildings. The Madeira cockroach is large (1½ inches to 2 inches) and is pale brown to tawny olive. This slow-moving adult cockroach actively flies. When it is disturbed, it emits a foul odor. Some people report that it even produces sounds. Imagine a smelly, noisy, flying cockroach!

3
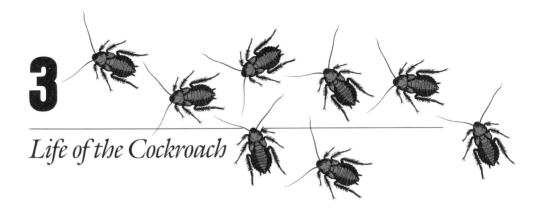

Life of the Cockroach

What's it like being a cockroach? In some respects, cockroaches have an easier life than kids. Cockroaches never have homework or spelling tests. They never have to share their toys or make their beds. (Of course, you must remember that cockroaches don't *have* toys or beds.) On the plus side, they can run really fast.

But the life of a cockroach is no bed of roses. If you were a cockroach, you would spend most of your life hiding in some crack. You would smell bad. What's more, you would always be at risk of giants (people) stepping on you—unless you lived in a remote place.

In this chapter, we will talk about the cockroach's enemies, what cockroaches eat, where they live, how they mate, and how their young develop.

Shelter

Pest cockroaches aren't that particular about where they live. They can survive cold and hot temperatures. They have survived trips to outer space in cola-can-size containers padded with only a small amount of cotton for protection. However, cockroaches prefer certain conditions.

Cockroaches flourish (1) when the air is moist, (2) when the temperature is between 52° F and 65° F (11° C and 18° C), and (3) when there is plenty of food and water. For these reasons, you can find thousands of pest cockroaches in restaurants, homes, offices, and sewers.

Cockroaches rest in one spot without moving for at least eighteen hours a day. They have a particular resting position. The antennae point upward and angle outward. The abdomen touches the surface, while the legs hold the body close to the surface. On the rear of the body, the cerci are slightly raised. Cockroaches don't care whether or not they rest sideways, or head up or down. They just like to be hidden. Often, only the antennae are visible.

During these eighteen hours, German cockroaches will group together in hiding. American cockroaches, on the other hand, are frequently found by themselves hanging on a dark wall. Wherever they hide, cockroaches leave a distinctive, disagreeable odor. Sometimes

Adult cockroaches sheltered
on a ledge in a cave

an exterminator can determine the type of cockroach infestation simply by taking a good whiff.

Food

When it gets dark, cockroaches leave their hiding places and look for food. For the next five or six hours, they are very active. Cockroaches eat only at night. If they don't find any food, they won't search during the day. Instead, they will wait until the following night.

Naturally, food and water are vital to cockroaches. Unless they have plenty of water, their hard bodies will dry up and they will die. But that is not to say that cockroaches must eat daily. In fact, they can go for a long time without food. Larger cockroaches can live longer than smaller ones. American cockroaches can live three weeks without food. With water, they can live a month. Smaller German cockroaches last two weeks without food and water.

Cockroaches are not picky eaters. Even though they will eat nearly anything—other cockroaches, food, books, glue, paper, clothing, fingernails, and the excrement of humans and animals—they *do* have favorite meals. Scientists have discovered that cockroaches enjoy (in order of preference): sugary cinnamon rolls, white bread, and boiled potatoes. They also enjoy bananas dipped in

37

38

beer. Cockroaches don't like bacon, hard-boiled eggs, or celery.

Young cockroaches (or nymphs) prefer different foods. They gain weight on dried beef steak, whole wheat and dried skim milk, whole wheat and dried blood, and ground meat. But when nymphs eat baby food, they don't gain very much weight at all.

Cockroaches' eating habits can be really disgusting. They may eat the cat's excrement from the litter box and then help themselves to your left-over supper on the kitchen table. Cockroaches vomit a portion of the food that they eat and they also liberally deposit their feces. Both leave a sickening smell. So, several hours later, if you were to eat the food that had been left out, guess what you'd be eating!

Not surprisingly, many scientists are convinced that cockroaches spread germs. They believe that cockroaches are carriers of infectious diseases such as salmonella (food poisoning), dysentery, diarrhea, Bubonic plague, leprosy, and typhoid fever. In addition, people who suffer from asthma or allergies are often allergic to cockroaches.

After dark, Oriental cockroaches gather at a local cafe to feast on cucumber sandwiches and drink coffee.

Cockroach eating popcorn

Traveling

Cockroaches are masters of escape. Although they can fly, they rarely use their wings. Most often, they use their lightning-speed legs. Cockroaches don't normally run long distances (although they do manage to travel thousands of miles by hiding on ships, planes, buses, trains, and cars. It's a much nicer way to travel, don't you think?). Nevertheless, scientists did record the track record of one cockroach in Tyler, Texas. This Texas cockroach left a manhole and made its way down the street to another manhole that was 385 yards (352 m) away. That's nearly four times the length of a football field.

Moreover, cockroaches have been known to swim. In fact, one way they can enter your home is by swimming through the sewer pipes which lead to the bathroom.

Occasionally, if conditions are not suitable, cockroaches will band together by the thousands and migrate. In the 1880s, people armed with brooms tried to prevent a horde of cockroaches from leaving a local restaurant and entering the nation's Capitol building. The people lost. By 1985, the cockroach problem was so severe in Washington, D.C., that Congressman Silvio Conte launched the "Conte Crush-a-Cockroach Campaign."

Natural Enemies

Cockroaches have many natural enemies. However, because they are so fast and because they hide during the day, their enemies can't always find them. It's possible

A mother cockroach
guards her newborn.

42

that animals are repulsed by their smell. Small animals such as frogs, lizards, birds, garter snakes, and mice will sometimes dine on cockroaches. Spiders, scorpions, and centipedes also eat cockroaches. Some wasps carry cockroaches to their nests as food for their larvae. Other wasps lay eggs in the egg sacs of cockroaches. The wasp eggs hatch first and eat up the cockroach eggs. Of course, cockroaches' principal enemies are humans. But we're not very good at capturing them.

Mating

One of the main reasons it is so difficult to control cockroaches is that they reproduce large numbers of young in a relatively short time. Some fifteen to forty nymphs can emerge in as little as three weeks. What's more, even if female cockroaches mate only one time, they can produce new sets of young for the rest of their lives.

When a female cockroach is ready to mate, she emits a pheromone, or a sexual attractant, which strongly excites a male cockroach. In response, his wings raise and flutter as he seeks the female. He grasps her, and at first, his body is under hers. If the copulation is going successfully, however, their positions will change and the two cockroaches will mate end to end. They will remain locked in this position for about an hour.

Two brown-banded cockroaches mating.
The female is on the left.

Ootheca

A few days after copulation, female cockroaches produce an ootheca, or egg sac. The ootheca protects the eggs so that they can grow and develop. Although the ootheca of German cockroaches remains attached to their bodies, most other female cockroaches deposit their ootheca in a hidden place. (One tropical species internalizes this process and gives birth to live young.) The eggs inside the ootheca are greatly dependent on the weather and will develop faster in warmer weather.

To hatch, the ootheca splits open and the nymphs emerge suddenly. These young cockroaches begin to move about immediately. They don't have wings and they are pale in color. Other than that, they look like adult cockroaches.

Molting

A nymph passes through six to twelve *molts* before it reaches adulthood. Molting occurs when a cockroach no longer fits inside its cuticle (the outer covering). Thus, the cuticle splits open and a slightly larger cockroach emerges with a new skin. A young cockroach will also regenerate lost body parts during a molt. So, if a cockroach loses a leg, antenna, cercus, or a mouth part, a new one will appear after the next molt.

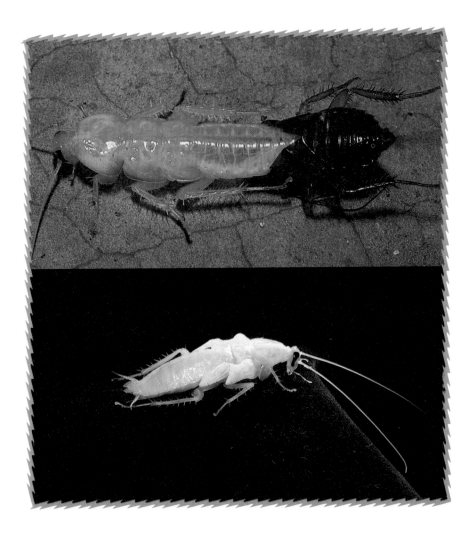

Facing page, from top: *German cockroach with ootheca; ootheca of Oriental cockroach on dried sycamore leaf; opened ootheca.* Above: *American cockroach nymph leaving old skin;* Below: *the white skin of the newly emerged adult will darken in a short period of time.*

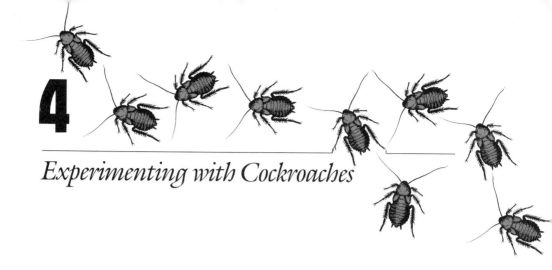

4

Experimenting with Cockroaches

In this book, you have learned about cockroaches' body parts, their activities, and the specific kinds of cockroaches. Now you are ready for some fun. Just like a real scientist, you are going to perform experiments on cockroaches.

Your first step is to get some cockroaches. Several companies sell cockroaches and materials. A few of these are listed on page 60. But there is a cheaper way to get some cockroaches. You can catch them yourself.

One way of catching cockroaches is by using traps. Use quart- or gallon-size jars. Smear a thin layer of petroleum jelly on the inside of the jar so that the cockroaches can not crawl out and escape. Place food in the jar. A good bait is a sugary cinnamon roll, white bread, or a boiled potato. Place the jars near walls and in corners of kitchens and basements—or any place that is near food and water.

A quicker way of catching cockroaches is with an insect net. (Of course, you can always use your hands, but be sure you wash them afterward.) After the sun has set, look for cockroaches in kitchens, near sewer coverings, or in stacks of firewood.

Don't kill the cockroaches that you catch. The experiments can't be performed with dead cockroaches. While they are in your care, treat them with respect.

House them in an empty aquarium. Spread some petroleum jelly around the top edges so that they can't crawl out. If you put a lid on the aquarium, make sure that the cockroaches have plenty of air.

Feed your cockroaches dry dog food and slices of apples, potatoes, and carrots. They also need fresh water. One way of providing it is to fill a test tube with water and cap it with a piece of wet cotton.

And above all, decorate your cockroaches' new home according to their own tastes. They like to hide under cardboard. So, make them a variety of cardboard shelters (see picture on page 50).

Basic Equipment

For your experiments, you will need some empty jars and a magnifying glass. Use plastic gloves or some old tweezers if you don't like to touch the cockroaches. *Always wash your hands with soap and water after you handle them.* If your eyes water or if you sneeze, you may be allergic to them. In that case, don't experiment. Instead, just read this chapter and imagine.

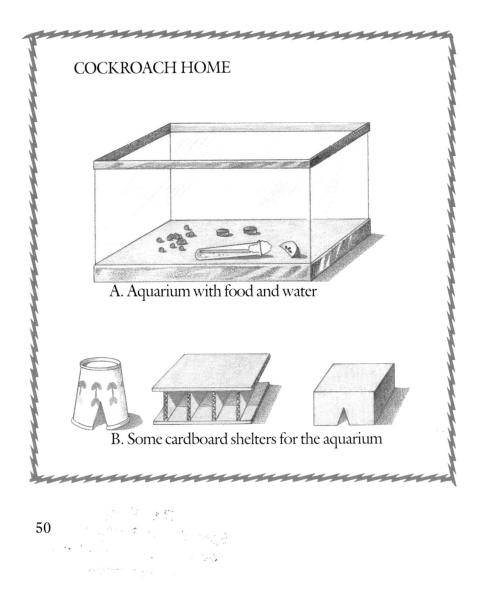

COCKROACH HOME

A. Aquarium with food and water

B. Some cardboard shelters for the aquarium

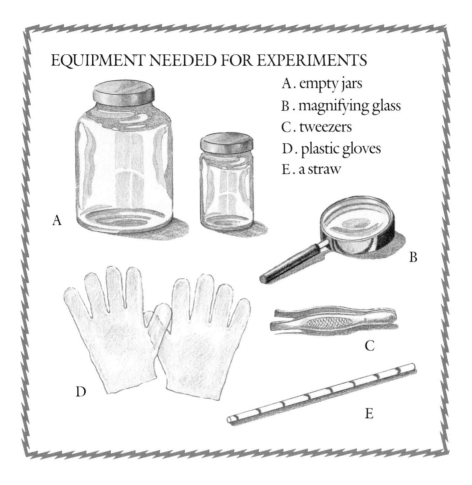

EQUIPMENT NEEDED FOR EXPERIMENTS

A. empty jars
B. magnifying glass
C. tweezers
D. plastic gloves
E. a straw

You will also need a cockroach arena. To make one, get two large pieces of poster board 22 (55 cm × 70 cm) by 28 inches. Cut one piece in half. These strips should measure 11 by 28 inches (27.5 cm × 70 cm). Staple or tape the edges together to make a circle. Place it on top of the other piece of poster board.

Experiment One:
Observation

Remove one cockroach from the aquarium and place it in a small jar. When you use your bare hands, do you feel the stiff hairs that are on the cockroach's legs? Do you feel the claws on its feet? The cockroach will probably run around the jar excitedly. Its antennae and palpi will be moving constantly. These help the cockroach taste and smell. After a while, the cockroach will calm down and remain in one spot. Notice that it will begin cleaning its legs, antennae, and other parts of its body. (The cockroach is washing because you touched it. Maybe it doesn't want your germs!)

Experiment Two:
Grooming

To get the cockroach to clean or groom itself, smear a light coat of honey and water on its body, legs, and antennae. Now watch the cockroach. Write down the steps of a cockroach bath. What part of the body does the cockroach groom first?

Repeat this process with several cockroaches. Do the cockroaches groom themselves the same way? How are they different? How are they alike?

Experiment Three:
Anatomy

In Chapter One, you learned the body parts of the cockroach. With your magnifying glass, you can see these parts for yourself. If you want the cockroach to be still during the examination, you can put it to sleep. To anesthetize a cockroach either (1) place it in the refrigerator for ten or fifteen minutes, or (2) immerse it in warm water for five minutes.

On the head, can you find the antennae, the eyes, and the palpi? Find the thorax. How many wings are there? Feel the stiff hairs on the legs. On the abdomen, locate the cerci. How long is the cockroach? What color is it? Is it fat or slender? What other things do you notice about the cockroach? Based on your observations, can you determine what kind of cockroach it is?

Experiment Four:
Righting Behavior

An important animal behavior is the animal's ability to turn itself over when it lands on its back. Gently drop a cockroach on its back in the arena. How does it right itself? Which legs are involved? Are the cockroach's actions the same each time you drop it?

Now drop the cockroach right side up on the glass surface of the aquarium. The smooth surface will slow down the cockroach's actions so that you can better observe the righting behavior.

Experiment Five:
Wall-seeking Behavior

Cockroaches protect themselves from enemies by staying close to corners and walls. To observe this behavior, drop a cockroach in the arena. Watch the insect for at least three minutes. How many times does it cross the middle of the arena? Does the cockroach stay close to the wall? Does the cockroach run at a steady pace or does it move in short bursts? Blow on the cockroach. Does it run to the edge or to the center?

Experiment Six:
Escape Behavior

Most predators produce a wind current when they attack a cockroach. When a rat lunges, when a toad flicks its tongue, or when a person walks into a kitchen, the cockroach feels the wind and flees from danger.

Simulate this escape behavior by placing a cockroach in the arena. Use a straw and blow puffs of air

EXPERIMENT SIX

360 degrees (in a full circle) around the cockroach. Does the cockroach respond? What does it do? Which organs are the most sensitive to the air currents?

Experiment Seven:
Response to Odors

For this experiment, you will need a piece of food, some water in a small container, and insecticide sprayed on a small piece of paper.

Place a cockroach in the arena. Put the piece of food in the center of the arena. Record the cockroach's pathways. Remove the food.

Repeat this process with the water and with the insecticide. What do you discover?

Experiment Eight:
Aggression

An animal will fight one of its own kind. It may fight over food, a mate, or suitable shelter. Animal fights determine which animal is the winner (the dominant) and which animal is the loser (the subordinate).

Aggression in cockroaches is more easily observed if you do the following:

Use American cockroaches, since they are more aggressive than German cockroaches.

Use male cockroaches since they are more aggressive than females.

Perform this experiment at night, when cockroaches are more active.

56

Use two cockroaches that have not previously met. Or, use two starved cockroaches and a piece of food.

Place the two cockroaches in the arena. There are five levels of aggression. Look at the actions of both cockroaches. Keep a score sheet and see if you can determine the winner.

Cockroach Score Sheet

Mark the number of times these actions are observed.

Fighting Level	Cockroach A	Cockroach B
Antennation*		
Rapid jerks of body Stilt-Walking†		
Biting, kicking		
Mutual biting, kicking		
Intensive grappling		

*Antennation means that one cockroach will touch the other cockroach with its antenna.

†Stilt-Walking means that one of the cockroaches will raise itself so that it will be taller than the other one.

Afterword

In 1916, Don Marquis, a writer for the *New York Sun*, described a curious event. He wrote that a cockroach by the name of Archy wrote poetry on his typewriter in the late evenings. Archy, Marquis declared, hurled himself against the keys with all his might. It was exhausting work. Archy wrote his poetry in lowercase letters because he was unable to hit the shift key and another key at the same time.

These poems, written by Marquis (alias Archy), became immensely popular. One poem began like this:

one thing the human
bean never seems to
get into it is the
fact that humans
appear just as unnecessary to
cockroaches as cockroaches
do to humans

I hope you have enjoyed reading about "dirty, disgusting, unnecessary" cockroaches. Even so, you don't have to love them. My wish is that you've learned something new and perhaps gained a small but definite respect for yet another living species that shares this wonderful and mysterious world with us.

Cockroach Suppliers

Cockroach Suppliers

BioQuip Products
P.O. Box 61
Santa Monica, CA 90406

Carolina Biological Supply Co.
2700 York Road Burlington, NC 27215

Connecticut Valley Biological Supply Co.
82 Valley Road, P.O. Box 326
Southampton, MA 01073

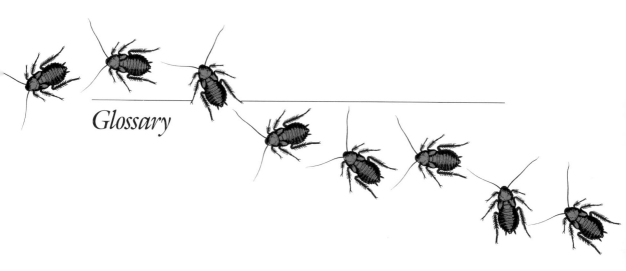

Glossary

Abdomen. Third, or last, section of the cockroach. Includes the heart, stomach, reproductive organs, and the cerci.

Antennae (singular: *antenna*). A pair of slender feelers located on the head and containing certain sense organs.

Blattaria. Suborder to which cockroaches belong, "blattaria" meaning "to shun the light."

Carboniferous period. Period of history that occurred some 300 million years ago, in which lush vegetation grew and, later in the period, rocks and coal beds were produced.

Cerci (singular: *cercus*). Pair of jointed sticklike feelers located on the rear of the abdomen and containing certain sense organs.

Crop. Organ where digestion occurs.

Fat body. White tissue that fills most of the cockroach's body; stores nutrients and secretes proteins to the blood.

Ganglia. Nerve cells.

Gut. Intestine.

Hindwings. The pair of wings that are underneath the *Tegmina*.

Mandibles. Mouth parts that are used to bite food.

61

Molt. The shedding of a coat, or outer covering.

Nymphs. Young wingless cockroaches after hatching.

Ootheca. Egg cases.

Ovipositor. An organ, located at the end of the female's abdomen, deposits eggs; organ is no longer external.

Palpi (singular: *palpus*). Jointed feelers attached to the mouth that are organs for touch and taste.

Proventriculus, or *gizzard.* A muscular organ posterior to the crop where the food is further ground up.

Spiracles. Tiny openings for breathing.

Sternites. Small, hard, overlapping segments on the underside of the abdomen.

Style. A pair of small, slender, pointed parts located on the end of the male's abdomen and on nymphs of both sexes.

Tegmina. The top pair of wings.

Tergites. Small, hard, overlapping segments on the topside of the abdomen, under the wings.

Thorax. Middle section of the cockroach, between head and abdomen, to which legs and wings are attached.

Ventral nerve cord. Long cord running from the head to the tail, which transmits sensory signals to all parts of the body.

Index